One amazing Sikh at a Time

Seerat Kaur Gill
Illustrated by Anantjeet Kaur

THE BROWSER
www.thebrowser.org
Publishers & Booksellers

Title: One Amazing Sikh at a Time

Author's Name: Seerat Kaur Gill

First Published in 2021 by:
JGS Enterprises Pvt Ltd
(Imprint The Browser)

Publisher's Address:
SCO 14-15, FF, Sector 8-C, Chandigarh 160 009
service@thebrowser.org

Edition: I
ISBN: 978-81-949542-9-3

Cover & layout design by Anantjeet Kaur

Printed at Thomson Press (India) Ltd.

THE BROWSER
www.thebrowser.org
Publishers & Booksellers

This book is dedicated to:

Anyone who appears different
Thinks differently
Views the world differently

We need more of you
You make the world

Infinitely better
Infinitely more colourful
Infinitely richer.

★ ★ ★ ★ ★

'Children are often afraid of being alone. In truth I think we're all afraid of being alone. In our hearts we all want to belong. Growing up, feeling like you're different can make those feelings of being alone and not belonging, even worse. I remember feeling like that. What children need to know is that being different is beautiful. We need to celebrate what makes us who we are, what makes us unique.
That is exactly what "One Amazing Sikh at a Time" does. It celebrates people for who they are. This is a book that'll help children see the beauty in being different. I would've loved to read a book like this when I was younger. I'm incredibly thankful to Seerat Kaur Gill and illustrator Anantjeet Kaur for sharing the gift of this book with all of us.'

– Jagmeet Singh, NDP national leader, Canada

★ ★ ★ ★ ★

'Someone rightly remarked that Sikhs are the most visible minority in the world. And I think. besides their appearance, their openness, sociability and vivacity makes them still more so. But some people only perceive them as soldiers and farmers. Seerat Kaur Gill in her beautiful book has revealed their wonderful latent colours and hues. They are painters, poets. singers, scientists. architects, actors, philanthropists, environmentalists. philosophers, martyrs, freedom fighters, generals, Maharajas and warriors of course. Anantjeet Kaur has very brilliantly illustrated the glory of all the faces in this gallery of glamour, pride and awe.
It is definitely a book for reading as well as keeping and presenting as a gift. I heartily congratulate Seerat for creating this wonderful book made out of her love for her people.'

– Surjit Patar, celebrated Punjabi poet

★ ★ ★ ★ ★

'I must congratulate Seerat on her first attempt to write short biographies of Sikh personalities, who achieved heights in their own fields. The young Punjabi populations living in foreign countries know little about heroes from their motherland, who enriched the culture and thoughts over a period. Future generations should take pride in associating with them. In this regard, the attempt of Seerat is praiseworthy.'

– Barjinder Singh Hamdard, Editor-in-Chief, Ajit Group

'Creative Writing runs in her blood. Her grandfather, Gurnam Singh Tir, was a celebrated satirist and her mother, Bubbu Tir, is a perceptive commentator on social issues. Seerat Kaur Gill is a versatile writer in her own right. Germane to her creative flair is her ability to spot the extraordinary in the ordinary humdrum of everyday life and spin it into a compelling narrative that at once is racy and nuanced. Seerat writes with a panache, whether it's on women-centric issues, walking the tightrope of parenting her two daughters through a millenial's eyes, or challenges in adapting to a tectonic shift.'

– Ramesh Vinayak, Senior Editor, Hindustan Times

'I was delighted to read a chapter on my grandfather Teja Singh Samundri, a legendary leader of the Gurdwara, social and educational reforms as well as India's freedom movement. The 51 illustrations in the book will reintroduce and familiarize the young with the rich heritage.'

– Taranjit Singh Sandhu, Ambassador of India, USA

CONTENTS

Preface

One day, my elder daughter, rushing back from school, said, 'Mama, let Papa not come to my school.' She spoke slowly, measuring each word before uttering it and gauging my reaction.

'Why not?' I asked her as gently as I could.

'My friends make fun of Papa because he's a Sardar.'

I would have been better prepared to pacify my little one, address her fears gently had we been living in the West or far from home. However, we were in Chandigarh – the capital of Punjab – home to colourful, turbaned Sardars, and beautiful *salwar-kameez* clad Sardarnis!

It took me some time to gain composure before I sat down with my daughter, cupped her hands in mine and told her that she should be proud of not just her turbaned father but every Sikh man and woman who lives by the ideals of this wonderful religion. But, of course, the child who had carelessly passed such a remark was not to blame. After all, he was all of five, but it was his environment, the people in his home, who probably felt that it was alright to poke fun at Sardars and their ilk.

After that, I began my quest, consciously acquainting both my daughters with Sikh men and women who had contributed to making the world more beautiful, more inspiring and certainly more colourful. What began as a quest for learning about famous Sardars (so that we could educate my daughter's classmate) began to take the shape of learning about famous Sikhs – both men and women. Some of them may not be practising Sikhs, but these brilliant Singhs and Kaurs have exhibited passion, worked hard and honed their talents to make this world a better place. It was a revelation for not just both my girls (Sehar Kaur and Mehreen Kaur) but for me as well. Our Sikh brethren rose above discrimination, racism and other struggles which come on account of being a minority but also overcame societal hostilities to carve their own niche.

ਬਾਬਾਣੀਆ ਕਹਾਣੀਆ ਪੁਤ ਸਪੁਤ ਕਰੇਨ ॥

"The stories of one's ancestors make the children good children."

–(Ang 951, Guru Granth Sahib)

One Amazing Sikh at a Time is a compilation of our bedtime stories – to learn about one amazing Sikh every night.

Here, I would also like to add that this book is not just for the Sikh readership. Rather it is for anyone and everyone who is looking for inspiration, who is curious about the Sikh faith and its followers, or who wants to know how achievers become who they are. It is as much for children as it is for their siblings, parents or grandparents.

It gives me a certain sense of pride that this book is a product of collaboration between two Kaurs – I have written it, but as Charlie Mackesy says, 'Pictures are like islands in a sea of words' – the exquisite illustrations are by Anantjeet Kaur.

I hope this is a book you can keep going back to.
I hope this is a book that can find a special place on your bookshelves.
I hope this is a book you can gift to someone.
I hope this is a book that can help pacify your child if the time comes.
But my biggest hope is that this will be a book because of which
you might not need to reassure your child.

— Seerat Kaur Gill

AMAR.SING

Amar Singh

The Top Cop / 6 Jun 1958 - Present

Once upon a time, there lived a boy in Malaysia called Amar. Malaysia is a small coastal country in Southeast Asia, having a sizeable Sikh population. During his growing years, Amar watched his grandfather and father, who were both policemen, wear their uniforms each morning. They looked quite handsome and commanding in their police uniforms. He, too, dreamt of joining the police force and wearing the smart, deep-blue uniform one day. When his grandfather passed away, all family members took away different things as keepsakes, but Amar decided to take the *lesung*, a mortar used for pounding spices in the kitchen. It was special because it had his grandfather's police authority number engraved on it.

Before joining the police force, Amar Singh studied a lot of different subjects. Knowledge removes fear and makes one brave and smart. So, the clever Amar went on to study law and criminal justice and to read about Shariah law and practice from different universities. Thereafter, he began his journey to become a brave and smart cop. Then, he joined the police as an Assistant Superintendent Cadet. Amar Singh rose to become Kuala Lumpur's chief of police and handled several high-profile cases. This amazing Singh earned the title of 'Singh is King' when he led raids on the ex-Prime Ministers' houses and investigated infamous scandals. The top cop worked tirelessly for 35 years.

'If you are doing something you love, you never work a day in your life,' he says matter-of-factly. Now retired, Amar Singh enjoys riding motorcycles. However, being a policeman will always remain his first love. 'If I have a chance to live my life all over again, I will still choose to be a police officer,' he says with a big grin.

"My grandfather was a police constable in the 1920s. My father joined the force in 1940s. So, with me in the police force as well, it has been a 90-year journey!"

Amrit Singh

The Courageous Lawyer / 1969 - Present

A couple had three daughters. Both the husband and wife had begun their careers as teachers. They believed in books and the power of education and often told their children that knowledge is power.

Their third born – Amrit Singh – grew up believing that knowledge can change the world. Therefore, she studied hard and went on to learn at some of the best schools in the world. She trained under great teachers at the University of Cambridge, the University of Oxford, and the Yale Law School. Not only hard-working and passionate, but Amrit was also a fierce and gritty girl. After finishing her studies, she began working as a civil rights lawyer in New York. Amrit Singh went on to join the American Civil Liberties Union and litigated cases on torture, indefinite detention, and post 9/11 discrimination. She was a strong critic of the torture and abuse of prisoners when Bush was the President of the United States of America.

Amrit now serves at the Open Society Justice Initiative. She litigates cases on national security and issues related to counterterrorism measures. 'The government cannot secretly detain and interrogate prisoners! I will continue my fight against torture and abuse,' the courageous Kaur says. She represents a new generation of amazing Sikh women who wield the law as a sword and shield on the civic battlefield. 'It does not matter which political party it is. My fight is for human rights and civil liberties, which is much above political affiliations,' she says with her characteristic tenacity. She may not have inherited her father's – the former Prime Minister of India, Dr. Manmohan Singh's – soft-spoken demeanour, but like him, she too continues to accomplish great things through the power of knowledge.

"The public have a right to know of policies and practices instituted by its government which led to the atrocities on the detainees."

Amrita Pritam

Doyenne of Punjabi Literature / 31 Aug 1919 - 31 Oct 2005

Little Amrit Kaur was the apple of her parents' eyes. Her father was a poet, scholar and editor of a literary journal. Maybe it was his genes, or a house full of books, or losing her mother at the young age of 11, or all of these which prompted Amrit to put pen to paper. So, she wrote and wrote to feel less lonely.

Soon after, the 16-year-old Amrit got married to editor Pritam Singh and changed her name. Amrita Pritam then went on to write several poems in the next decade, starting with romantic poems. Later, she joined the Progressive Writers' Movement and began writing on the socio-economic concerns of her times in the form of poetry. In those days, the partition of India had greatly disturbed her. Amrita had to move from Lahore to Dehradun. She carried the pain of the partition with her and began to write about the saga extensively, both in story and prose form. Amrita Pritam became the voice of the victims.

Amrita also greatly felt the pain of women suffering in silence due to neglect and suppression. She would often say, 'There are many stories which are not on paper. They're written in the bodies and minds of women.' In those times, when women were supposed to follow orthodox societal norms whether they agreed or not, Amrita Pritam decided to walk out of her marriage because it was devoid of love. She defiantly said, 'Love is more important than a marriage certificate.' The revolutionary Amrita practised what she preached – she found love with the painter Imroz and chose to live with him till death did them apart. After all, families are not always husband, wife, parents, and children. Families are any place where one feels safe, loved, respected, and supported.

At the ripe age of 86, Amrita Pritam passed away in her sleep. However, her amazing work continues to live in the hearts and minds of literature lovers around the world.

"When a man denies the power of women, he is denying his own subconscious."

Amrita Sher-Gil

The Alluring Artist / 30 Jan 1913 - 5 Dec 1941

This is a story about a beautiful baby girl, Amrita Sher-Gil, who was born to Marie Antoinette Gottesmann and Umrao Singh, in Budapest, Hungary. Her father, Umrao Singh Sher-Gil Majithia, was a Sikh aristocrat, and a learned scholar in Sanskrit and Persian. Due to financial problems, when the family moved to Shimla, India, Amrita was nine years old. She began learning piano and violin there. Amrita, and her younger sister, would hold concerts at Shimla's Gaiety Theatre during those days.

All along, Amrita also continued to pursue her passion – painting. She would even paint the domestic helpers at home! She received formal lessons in art and later studied at an art school in Florence. Her oil painting, **Young Girls**, won a gold medal in the year 1932 at the Paris Salon art show. However, Amrita Sher-Gil longed to go back to India. 'Europe belongs to Picasso, Matisse, Braque... India belongs only to me...', she would say. She felt that her destiny as a painter lay there. Back in India, Amrita rediscovered the magic of Mughal and Pahari schools of painting. She was also intrigued by the cave paintings at Ajanta. Strong, individualistic, sometimes melancholic women became Amrita's favourite subjects. They can be spotted in her paintings, such as the **Group of Three Girls** (1935), **Bride's Toilet** (1937), **Village Scene** (1938) and **The Little Girl in Blue** (1934). These works were later declared as National Art Treasures by the government of India.

Lahore, being a major cultural and artistic centre, truly inspired the young, creative Amrita. When you live in a place where people love what you do as much as you love it, it helps you polish your talent at a young age. So, Amrita painted through joy and sorrow at her Lahore studio, then in undivided India. Unfortunately, a few days before her solo art show in Lahore, Amrita became sick and passed away on 5th December 1941.

In mere 28 years of her life, Amrita Sher-Gil became a beacon of hope and pride for fellow women, artists and Sikhs across the globe.

"As soon as I put foot on Indian soil, my painting underwent a change in subject, spirit and technique."

Anarkali Kaur Honaryar

The Plucky Humanitarian / 1985 - Present

A long time ago, in the year 1521, Guru Nanak visited Afghanistan during his fourth journey, also called *udasi*, to sow seeds of his teachings. Today, nearly 500 years later, a Sikh girl continues to spread His message of humanitarianism and love in the land of the Afghans.

Anarkali was born to a Sikh family in Afghanistan. She grew up in very difficult times. Afghanistan was at war in the early 1990s, and there was no stable government. Despite the turbulence and bleak future, little Anarkali had big dreams. She dreamt of becoming a pilot one day.

Her parents supported her education, despite the looming threat of the Taliban forces. The Taliban believed in treating women unfairly by forcing them to wear a *burqa*, a garment covering the whole body, at all times, and not allowing them to work or study beyond a specific age. However, Anarkali's parents supported their daughter's dream of studying and working.

After finishing school, she decided to join Kabul University to study dentistry. She grew up to become Dr Anarkali through hard work and perseverance. As a dentist, she reached out to people and became popular as a social activist. She particularly helped women who suffered from domestic abuse, gender discrimination, and forced marriages. Dr Anarkali may not have become a pilot, but she gifted wings to many others. Her efforts were recognised, and she won several awards for promoting tolerance and non-violence in a place rife with extremism.

It may be easy to suppress people with the power of a gun, but it is impossible to stop an empowered woman from doing great things. Anarkali Honaryar continues to keep Guru Nanak's teachings alive by walking on the path paved by Him centuries ago. She is a symbol of the equality, love and peace that Nanak had preached about long ago. This feisty Kaur is, indeed, shouldering the responsibility with aplomb.

"I am the daughter of ancestors who embraced Sikhism when Guru Nanak set foot on the land of Afghanistan."

ARJAN SINGH

Arjan Singh

Astounding Air Marshal / 15 Apr 1919 - 16 Sept 2017

Kishan Singh Aulakh and Kartar Kaur of Lyallpur, then in British India, were blessed with a son and named him Arjan Singh. He grew up on his grandfather's farm, where he spent his childhood watching planes, and dreaming of flying one, someday.

His dream began taking shape when the young Arjan joined the Royal Air Force College in Cranwell, England. Arjan was commissioned as a pilot officer after his training and went on to become the commander of No. 1 Squadron. Arjan Singh was a dynamic and fearless pilot. Once, while trying to raise the morale of a trainee pilot, Squadron Leader Arjan Singh conducted a dangerously low-level air pass over a house in Kerala. He could have been tried in court for such an action, but he sternly refuted charges saying, 'Such tricks are needed for every cadet to be a fighter pilot.' It was hard to not agree with him. After all, Air Force officers would have to be prepared for difficult flights and saving people at the same time.

The dashing, turbaned flyer went on to serve as the Chief of Air Staff from 1964 to 1969. To honour his contribution in the 1965 Indo-Pakistan war, he was also awarded the Padma Vibhushan, the second-highest civilian award in India. In 2002, he was promoted as the Marshal of the Indian Air Force, the highest rank in the Indian Air Force, which is held for life.

The little boy who would intently watch airplanes from his grandfather's farm went on to fly 65 different types of aircraft and continued to fly planes till the last day of his retirement. At times, we find our calling quite early in life. The trick is to hold on to it no matter what everybody else says, feed it with hard work and passion, and follow it with complete faith and dedication.

"He's 95 and still cracks a better salute than anyone I've ever seen."
– (Shiv Aroor, Senior Editor, India Today)

Arpana Caur

The Storyteller Artist / 4 Sept 1954 - Present

A little girl from Delhi, Arpana, grew up watching, listening, and absorbing art, culture, and literature. She was strongly influenced by her writer-mother. Women and their role in society always intrigued her. Little Arpana watched Amrita Sher-Gil's paintings with great awe. She loved how the women in Amrita's paintings used to come alive! As a young nine-year-old, Arpana tried to emulate women in Amrita's paintings in her own oil painting and named it **Mother and Daughter**.

When Arpana went to college, she studied literature, but her heart remained in painting. When one is sure of where one's heart lies, one always finds a way to get there. That is how the journey of Aparna Caur – the artist – began. Her journey was unique in many ways. She spelt her surname 'Caur' with a 'C' instead of the conventional 'K'. She inherited this distinctiveness from her writer-mother, the self-proclaimed black sheep in a family of doctors. Arpana began learning to paint on her own. The literature she read, the Pahari paintings she loved, the women she grew up among, became her inspiration. Arpana's paintings are famously known for seamlessly playing before one's eyes, just like poetry. Spirituality, time and nature are themes which often recur in Arpana's paintings. She loves big canvases. 'I want my entire inner world to reflect on the canvas!' she says. Despite the lack of space in art galleries and fewer buyers, she continued to paint on life-size canvases.

Stories of great people are built on the shoulders of other great ones who have dared to do wonderful things in life. In this case, it was Amrita Sher-Gil who inspired Arpana and paved the path for her to create her own niche as an artist. Who knew the storyteller-artist would one day exhibit her works in all corners of the world? Be it the Museum of Modern Art in New Delhi, Mumbai, Düsseldorf, Singapore, Bradford, or London's Albert Museum, or San Francisco's Asian Art Museum, the nine-year-old who drew **Mother and Daughter** has come a long, long way.

"When my paintings are hung in museums abroad, they say 'I am an Indian painting'."

Baba Deep Singh

The Valiant Warrior / 26 Jan 1682 - 11 Nov 1757

On the day of Baisakhi in 1699, a young boy named Deep, from the Pahuwind village in Amritsar district, went to Anandpur Sahib and got ceremonially inducted into Khalsa by Guru Gobind Singh. That day marked an important event in the life of Deep Singh. He began to learn weaponry, hunting and horsemanship. He even learnt to read and write in Gurmukhi and played an important role in helping Bhai Mani Singh make hand-written copies of the scripture of Guru Granth Sahib.

Baba Deep Singh was a brave warrior. In April 1757, the Afghani invader, Ahmad Shah Durrani had demolished the Golden Temple in Amritsar, and had filled the sacred pool with bodies of slaughtered animals. Baba Deep Singh, who was then 75 years old, took a vow to avenge the disrespect shown to the most important pilgrimage site of the Sikhs. This led to the Battle of Amritsar in 1757 against Prince Timur Shah, the second ruler of the Durrani empire, and his powerful army. Baba Deep Singh fought valiantly in the war; unfortunately, he became mortally wounded on the neck. Nevertheless, he braved the wound and continued to fight the enemy and breathed his last on reaching the periphery of Harmandir Sahib. The 15 kg double-edged sword, called the *Khanda*, which he used in his final battle, is preserved at the Akal Takht, in the Harmandir Sahib complex in Amritsar.

Baba Deep Singh's life is a testimony to the life of a Khalsa. More than just embracing the five signs – *Kangha* (comb), *Kara* (steel bangle), *Kesh* (uncut hair), *Kirpan* (short sword) and *Kachhehra* (short trousers) – it is about standing up for the Sikh ideals, even if it means giving up your life for them.

ਜਉ ਤਉ ਪ੍ਰੇਮ ਖੇਲਣ ਕਾ ਚਾਉ ॥ ਸਿਰੁ ਧਰਿ ਤਲੀ ਗਲੀ ਮੇਰੀ ਆਉ ॥

Jao Tao Prem Khelan ka Chao. Sir Dhar Tali Gali Meri Aao.

"Those who wish to play the game of love (to follow the Sikh path), come to me with your head in your palm."
– (Ang 1412, Guru Granth Sahib)

Balbir Singh Dosanjh

Golden Hat-trick Gentleman / 31 Dec 1923 - 25 May 2020

It all began with a young fellow playing hockey on the grounds of his college in Lahore. Harbail Singh, the hockey coach from the Khalsa College in Amritsar, watched closely as the lanky Sardar wielded his hockey stick like it was a magic wand! 'Come with me to Amritsar; I will train you. I can see that you will be a hockey star,' said the coach. The name of the promising hockey player was Balbir Singh.

Balbir began training and practising with Harbail Singh. The hockey stick became his constant companion. He would even eat and sleep with it by his bedside! From university matches to national championships, Balbir readied himself for the Olympics. It was in 1948 during the London Olympics, when Balbir Senior, as he began to be fondly called to distinguish him from the other hockey player named Balbir, tasted gold. Four years later, during the Helsinki Olympics, he earned his second gold by scoring a hat-trick against Great Britain. His third gold medal came when he beat Pakistan during the Melbourne Olympics in 1956.

Soft-spoken and dedicated towards his sport, Balbir Singh was a legend. His magic wand was his hockey stick, and he swung it with passion when he played for his country. 'For the first time in 1948, the tricolour was hoisted on the top. As the flag was going up, I felt as if I was going up too. Then I realised, no, I am on the ground. I still remember how it felt, as if I was going up as well. I felt as if I was flying,' he fondly remembered on returning from his first Olympics game in London.

When Balbir Senior played hockey, he played for all his countrymen, irrespective of what they looked like or which god they worshipped. That was his amazing super power – he united everyone with the wand and magic of his hockey stick!

"It was a proud moment for all of us when we defeated England, which had, until a year ago, ruled India for a long period, on their turf (in 1948)."

Balbir Singh Seechewal

The Eco Warrior / 2 Feb 1962 - Present

Balbir was born in the village of Seechewal in the Jalandhar district of Punjab. Like most of the village boys and girls, Balbir too went to the nearby college in Nakodar to study arts. One day, on the bus ride to college, he met Sant Avtaar Singh, the chief of an organisation that worked for public welfare and spread messages of Gurbani. Balbir became his disciple, and started working for his organisation, basing his life on one motto: 'Let us work ourselves to better our lives'.

He set out to first create roads in and around his village. He also installed the first sewerage system in his area. 'For how long should I wait for the government to provide us with fundamental amenities?' he would often say when people asked him why he was doing the state's job himself.

His efforts led to economic prosperity and inspired the growth of schools and colleges in the area. However, this was just the beginning of a huge revolution that Balbir Singh Seechewal would become synonymous with. Seechewal transformed a filthy drain into a healthy rivulet brimming with life and flowing into Sutlej and Beas rivers. It took him nearly 16 years to rejuvenate this rivulet, called **Kali Bein**, where Guru Nanak attained enlightenment. Balbir Singh was honoured with the Padma Shri for this commendable achievement. Today, the riverbank has become a picturesque picnic spot, with bathing areas and brick roads. Seechewal also developed a cost-effective underground sewerage system that treats water and provides clean water for irrigation, besides running a forest nursery.

This amazing 'Eco Baba' is today well-known for his efforts towards taking care of the environment. The *Japji Sahib* says that 'Air is the Guru, Water the Father, and the Earth is the Great Mother'. *Sant* Balbir Singh Seechewal's super power was to embrace wholeheartedly the wonderful teachings of religion along with science, and thus create a happy future on planet Earth.

"Water is life. If there's no water, there's nothing left for mankind."

BANA SINGH

Bana Singh

The Sturdy Soldier / 6 Jan 1949 - Present

Not long ago, in the Kadyal district of Jammu province in India, there lived a young boy called Bana. His father would often tell him, 'Son, life is harsh for a farmer like me. When you grow up, you must join the prestigious army.' Bana grew up listening to his father, and watching his uncles serve in the Indian Army.

Some 20 years later, Bana Singh enrolled in the Indian Army, and began his training at the High Altitude Warfare School in Gulmarg. He learnt about mountain warfare, mountain climbing, fighting in low visibility caused by snow, and mobility in a glacier. He was being trained to be deployed on the Siachen glacier, the highest battleground in the world between India and neighbouring Pakistan.

It was in June 1987 when Singh volunteered to be a part of the task force that had been constituted to clear an intrusion in the Siachen glacier area. It was snowing heavily, and the visibility was extremely low. In an operation that lasted nearly five hours, the brave Singh managed to lead his team through a challenging route, wherein they had to crawl through trenches, dodge hand grenades, and fight the adversaries. *Naib Subedar* Bana Singh captured the Quaid Post, which was renamed as **Bana Top** in honour of the gallant soldier.

People often ask him, 'Did you feel scared fighting the enemy in such cold, adverse conditions?' The fearless Param Vir Chakra awardee and Honorary Captain Bana Singh promptly says,

***"When you face death,
you don't feel cold, you don't feel fear."***

In such tough times, amazing Sikhs like Bana Singh draw strength from their inner selves because they know that only when one overcomes one's fear, real growth happens.

Bawa Kartar Singh

The Stereo Chemist / 17 Apr 1886 - 15 Jun 1960

In the far-flung village of Vairowaal in Amritsar, a baby boy was born to Bawa Jiwan Singh. He named his son Bawa Kartar Singh. Kartar inherited a keen academic interest from his father, who was a member of Indian Medical Services in those days. He, too, went on to crack the medical entrance examinations and won a meritorious rank at the Calcutta University. This achievement was only the beginning of many firsts in Kartar's life.

Bawa Kartar Singh went on to study at the Cambridge University in the UK. After finishing his studies and returning to India, he began teaching as a professor of chemistry. Being surrounded by people who inspire can propel one to achieve one's highest potential in life. This is what happened when Bawa Kartar Singh came in touch with Sir P.C. Ray and Dr Watson. He began his research journey at the Government College in Lahore with them. Sitting in his laboratory, he would often wonder, 'How are atoms arranged to form molecules? Is it possible to change their arrangement?' He established relationships between optical activity and the chemical constitution of compounds. He began to be called the '**Father of Stereo Chemistry**' because of his research achievements. This exciting research journey took Dr Bawa Kartar Singh to universities across India, where he taught and shared his knowledge with young minds.

This super-scientist was one of the ten Indians who was asked to send their proposal for the Nobel Prize in chemistry. Although his submission was not successful, this amazing son of Punjab will globally be remembered for his contributions to the world of chemistry.

"The Nobel Foundation would do well, if they were to assist in the development of pharmacological studies in laboratories devoted to synthetic organic chemical work in the different parts of the world."
—(Bawa Kartar Singh's Nobel Prize Nomination Letter of Recommendation)

Bhagat Puran Singh

The Humble Humanitarian / 4 Jun 1904 - 5 Aug 1992

More than a century ago there lived in Rajewal a young boy called Ramji Das in the Ludhiana district of Punjab. He had a comfortable life; his father was a wealthy moneylender. Ramji was particularly close to his mother. She instilled in her young son the Sikh ideals of living, such as humanity, selfless service, love and compassion for humans and animals. Moved by her teachings, Ramji embraced Sikhism and began to be called *Bhagat* Puran Singh, a word that means a saint.

Bhagat Puran Singh decided that he would selflessly work in the service of humanity. He began his mission from the streets of Lahore. On spotting an injured or physically handicapped person, he would rush to his aid. He would also take the sick to the hospital and get them treated.

It was on a dark night in 1934 when Bhagat Puran Singh found a four-year-old child outside the gurudwara. The unfortunate child was mentally and physically impaired, and suffered from an acute intestinal infection. This incident marked an important event in the life of Bhagat Puran Singh. He cleaned the child and began taking care of him. This was the beginning of a fourteen-year-old association with the young child, whom he named Piara. Bhagat would carry Piara on his back every day for the next fourteen years, and would fondly call him the 'garland around his neck'. After the partition of India in 1947, Bhagat Puran Singh settled in Amritsar, where he continued his selfless service. People began to notice. Donations started pouring in to support Bhagat in his noble endeavours. The Government of Punjab also provided him with land to build a shelter. Bhagat Puran Singh then founded **Pingalwara**, a house for the destitute in Amritsar.

When the amazing Bhagat Puran Singh passed away, his belongings were so few that they could be counted on one hand. However, he left behind a legacy of humility and the spirit of selflessness. The Pingalwara Charitable Society continues to work on Bhagat Puran Singh's principles worldwide.

"Dignity in death is a birthright of each living being."

ਕੁਦਰਤ ਦੀ
ਰਚਨਾ ਵਿਚੋਂ,
ਸੁਹਣੇ,

Bhai Vir Singh

The Father of Modern Punjabi Literature / 5 Dec 1872 - 10 Jun 1957

It was a cold December morning in Amritsar. A baby boy was born in the illustrious Dr Charan Singh's house. Named Vir Singh, he grew up learning the Sikh scripture and several languages, including English, Persian, Urdu and Sanskrit.

As a young boy, Vir would often wonder what he wanted to do in life. The power of books always lured him because they had ideas, and ideas could change the world. When Vir Singh began penning down his ideas, he realised that writing was his true calling. Around the same time, some of Vir Singh's Sikh friends in Church Mission High School converted to Christianity. 'I need to revitalise Sikh culture and win back my dispirited friends!' he determinedly thought. Vir Singh strongly felt that this could be done through literature.

Novels, epics, and poems, he decided, could be powerful mediums to revive Sikhism. It was with this intention that Bhai Vir Singh began to write books, which became widely appreciated and loved. Far ahead of his time, he wrote classics reflecting strong female characters such as **Sundari** (1898), **Bijay Singh** (1899), **Rana Surat Singh** (1919), **Satwant Kaur** (1927), and **Mere Saiyan Jiyo** (1953). In the years to come, Vir Singh, through the sheer magic of his pen, inspired, besides many others, the then disillusioned Puran Singh, who, like Bhai Vir Singh, also went on to create iconic Sikh literature.

ਉੱਚਾ ਉਠ ਜ਼ਮੀਨ ਤੋਂ ਪਿਆਰੇ / *Ucha uth zameen ton pyare*
ਤੈਨੂੰ ਖੰਭ ਰੱਬ ਨੇ ਲਾਏ / *tenu khamb rabb ne laye.*
ਉਹ ਕਿਓਂ ਰਿੜ੍ਹੇ ਗੋਡਿਆਂ ਪਰਨੇ / *oh kyon rirhe godeyaan parne?*
ਜੋ ਉੱਡ ਅਸਮਾਨੀ ਜਾਏ / *jo udd asmani jaaye*

"Get up, get off the floor, dear one
God has bestowed you with wings
Why do you crawl on your knees
When you can take flight and soar high?"

Bibi Bhagbhari

The Progressive Prelate / Late 1400s - Early 1500s

In 1614, Bhai Madho Sodhi was sent to Kashmir by Guru Arjun Dev to preach Sikhism. A young woman, belonging to a Brahmin family of Srinagar, called *Bibi* Bhagbhari, became greatly influenced by the Sikh principles. She converted to Sikhism and began to further tell people in and around Kashmir about the wonderful faith and its tenets.

Bibi Bhagbhari began to preach and teach Sikhism with dedication and hard work. Her sincerity led her to be given a seat or *manji* in the Sikh administrative system to propagate the Sikh faith and its teachings in Kashmir. Her role was similar to that of a bishop-mayor. She advocated the three pillars of Sikhism – earn an honest living (*Kirat Karo*), meditate on God's name (*Naam Japo*), and share your good fortune (*Vand Chhako*), as well as managed the local community.

As Bhagbhari aged, her son, Seva Das continued her duties. Although content, she longed to have a glimpse of the Guru. By then, Guru Hargobind had occupied the spiritual throne. Bhagbhari had stitched a beautiful robe made of homespun fabric, and desired to present it to the Guru. Soon after, Guru Hargobind travelled to Kashmir, and paid a visit to Bibi Bhagbhari's house at the Hathi Gate area in Srinagar.

Seeing the Guru, Bibi Bhagbhari was euphoric with happiness. She fulfilled her wish by presenting the robe to the Guru and passed away peacefully. Her life was a testimony of not only her belief in Sikhism as a faith but also the unsung, important role that Sikh women have played throughout history.

ਸਤਗੁਰੁ ਦਇਆ ਕਰੇ ਸੁਖਦਾਤਾ ਹਮ ਲਾਵੈ ਆਪਨ ਪਾਲੀ ॥

Satgur Daya Karey Sukhdata, Hum Laavai Aapan Paali

"If the True Guru, the Giver of Peace, shows his kindness, He attaches us to the hem of His robe."
– (Ang 667, Guru Granth Sahib)

Diljit Dosanjh

The Punjabi Pop-Icon / 4 Jan 1984 - Present

Once, there was a young boy, Daljit, from village Dosanjh Kalan in the Jalandhar district of Punjab, who would often perform *Kirtan* at the local gurudwara. Full of life, little Daljit would be seen at every single wedding and birthday party in his village. Irrespective of whether he was invited or not, the little boy would dance and sing like no one was watching him and would participate in everyone's happiness.

Soon after, Daljit was sent to the city of Ludhiana to pursue his first love – singing. He began by first learning how to play musical instruments such as the *tabla* and the harmonium. Thus, began Daljit's singing career. At the suggestion of a producer, Daljit changed his name to Diljit, as it sounded unique.

People loved Diljit's singing style. Gradually, he stepped into the world of Punjabi movies and was appreciated for his fine acting skills. Many, many more milestones awaited him. He began to be offered big Bollywood movies as well, but on the condition that he would have to lose his turban! Diljit was warned that people might not want to watch a turbaned man in Bollywood movies. However, he did not want to become a star by losing his identity. At times, it seems easier to please people than to be your true self. Diljit's super power, though, was to remain authentic, even if it meant not being able to become a famous actor.

'I will work in movies, and I will also flaunt my turban, and people will love me even more,' he said. True to his words, Diljit became supremely popular, and people could not get enough of the talented turbaned man! Diljit Dosanjh has become a recognisable face in Bollywood today.

This amazing Singh may have earned global stardom in the world of entertainment and movies, but deep down, he is the simple, happy-go-lucky boy from Dosanjh Kalan who still cherishes the endless buckets of sweet sherbet, as he did in his childhood!

"I owe everything to Punjabi cinema."

Dyal Singh Majithia

The Progressive Philanthropist / 1848 - 9 Sept 1898

A long time ago, there lived an extraordinary man, called Lehna Singh, in the city of Benares. His son, Dyal Singh, was like him. He learnt from his father the importance of self-education. People admired Dyal for his scientific knowledge, foresightedness and diplomatic finesse.

After having spent two years abroad, Dyal Singh realised the important role played by an independent press. 'We need our own press – an English newspaper in Lahore,' he thought. It was a revolutionary idea at that time. So Dyal Singh founded the iconic newspaper, ***The Tribune***, on returning to Lahore, which did not mince words in exposing the misgovernance of the British Raj. It was a bold and fearless newspaper, which also played an important role in the freedom struggle.

Besides *The Tribune*, Dyal Singh also launched the first Punjabi bank called the **Punjab National Bank**. Majithia was the main force behind the University of Punjab in undivided Punjab as well. He donated many of his properties to set up institutions that played a vital role in nation-building. The wealthy aristocrat could have enjoyed his riches and lived an easy life of luxury, but he wanted to contribute to society in a bigger way and used his money and properties to create enduring institutions. Dyal Singh Majithia made three trusts – The Tribune Trust, the Dyal Singh College Trust, and Dyal Singh Public Library. The partition led to the shifting of these trusts from Lahore in Pakistan to Majitha in Amritsar, Karnal, and New Delhi in India.

A progressive mind always takes the society forward. Dyal Singh strongly believed in inclusiveness and would enthusiastically say, 'Down with the shams and hypocrisies, pull down the false gods, march with the times, create a new India!' Dyal Singh Majithia, a gem of the nineteenth century, played a very important role in modernising Punjab. Despite the partition of India, his amazing legacy lives on through the commendable institutions he created during his lifetime.

"The progress and liberation of the Punjabis can only happen through education."

Fateh Kaur

The Peacemaker / Unknown - 1773

This is a story from a long time ago, when a daughter was born to a couple in Sangrur, Punjab. The parents were disappointed on the birth of a girl and decided to put the baby in an earthen vessel and bury her alive! A man named Dyal Das was passing by. He noticed a woman crying inconsolably.

'What has caused you so much grief, *bibi*?' he inquired gently.

Through her tears, she told him that she was guilty of burying her baby girl. He convinced her to dig out the helpless child and welcome her with love. Fortunately, the little girl was still alive and was taken home by her mother. The parents named the resilient child Fateh Kaur.

Fateh Kaur, lovingly called Fatto, grew up to be a strong, loving girl. She was married to Baba Ala Singh, the founder of the state of Patiala. In 1761, when the abominable Afghan invader, Ahmad Shah Durrani, was heading back to Kabul after the Battle of Panipat, he looted and plundered cities and towns on his way back. Maaee Fatto was a worldly-wise woman. She knew how to use her words to her advantage. She negotiated with Ahmad Shah and helped secure peace in the state. Her influence also helped her husband in garnering support from respected Sikh families in Punjab.

Counted as one of the builders of the Patiala state, Fateh Kaur peacefully passed away in 1773 and was then befittingly buried in the royal cemetery called *Shahi Samadhan*. If her parents had succumbed to societal pressures many years ago and lost their baby girl, history would have been different. When more mothers and fathers stand up against the evils of society, the world will be full of amazing, courageous women like Fateh Kaur.

"They buried us, but they didn't know we were seeds." – (Dinos Christianopoulos, Greek post-war poet and novelist)

Gagandeep Kaur Kang

The Vaccine Godmother / 3 Nov 1962 - Present

Francoise Barré, the famous scientist, once said, 'Certain people – men, of course – discouraged me, saying science was not a good career for women. That pushed me even more to persevere.' There have been few women scientists, not because women are any less capable, but because they lack necessary support, such as being able to work flexible hours or shift jobs. However, today, Barré and many others from the scientific community have a reason to rejoice and celebrate.

When a young Gagandeep Kaur, from Jalandhar, in Punjab, started her career as a doctor, she decided that one day she would improve the vaccines for Indian children. So, this super scientist set on a mission to fight diarrhoea, a common bacterial infection of the stomach among children. She worked in her laboratory day in and day out. Gagandeep also collaborated with other scientists to understand infections among children and helped in developing vaccines against rotavirus and typhoid.

Her extensive work and achievements in the scientific field paid off, and biologist Gagandeep Kaur Kang became the first Indian woman to be inducted as a Fellow of the Royal Society in 2019 in its history of 359 years. On being asked if there were any other powers that she wished she had, she replied with her characteristic smile, 'Stretching time! There is too much to do in India and other similar places, but not enough people, and not enough time!'

Just like the fairy godmother in Cinderella, Gagandeep Kaur Kang is a real-life vaccine godmother. Only instead of pumpkins and animals, she has a laboratory and science books!

"I can't wait for the day when more and more women researchers fill positions and black swans become the norm."

Gulab Kaur

The Resolute Revolutionary / 1890 - 1931

Once upon a time, there was a gritty girl from the Bakshiwala district in Sangrur, Punjab called Gulab Kaur. She, along with her husband, moved from India to the Philippines, and thereafter to the United States of America in search of a better life for themselves. There, she met some people affiliated with the Ghadar Party. This party had begun as a movement among Indians, particularly the Sikhs living in North America, against oppression. Gulab Kaur, too, became motivated by the ideals of the Ghadar Party. 'I will work for the party. I will take care of printing and distributing party literature,' she announced before formally joining the Ghadar Revolution.

She bravely posed as a press journalist and helped the Ghadarites to procure arms. Soon after, Gulab Kaur began to be recognised for her contributions and was called ***Ghadar di dhee*** (The Daughter of the Ghadar Revolution). This valiant Kaur would often be seen giving fiery speeches on boats to Indian passengers, inspiring them to join the freedom cause.

Over time, Gulab Kaur left her husband to devote herself completely to the cause of Ghadar Party. She decided to go back to India to participate in the struggle to overthrow the British Government. As soon as she reached India, this feisty revolutionary was arrested and tortured at Lahore's Shahi Qila. Gulab Kaur died in 1931; however, she will be remembered till eternity as the Daughter of the Ghadar Revolution – the amazing woman who gave up everything, even her marriage, for this cause. In an era when women had strictly defined domestic roles, revolution became Gulab Kaur's trailblazing contribution to the world.

"Freedom is not for the timid."
– (Vijaya Lakshmi Pandit)

Gurdas Maan

The Man with a Golden Voice / 4 Jan 1957 - Present

In the sleepy town of Gidderbaha in Shri Muktsar Sahib district of Punjab, Tej Kaur would sing songs to her little son, Gurdas, to lull him to sleep. Little did she know that one day, he would sing ***Mawaan Thandiyaan Chhaawan*** (mothers are safe shelters) for her, and the whole world would sing with him.

This is the story of Gurdas Maan – the man with a golden voice. As he grew up, he began to write songs, give them his soulful voice and make magical music. His music had the aroma of Punjab. The special thing about Gurdas Maan's music was that it told several stories. Some were painful and spoke of the Partition and suffering during the 1984 riots. Others were happy ones based on the joyfulness of a child and the limitless potential of the youth. There were foot-tapping stories about mustard fields, blue skies, gushing tube wells and the beautiful state of Punjab as well. Everybody began to love Maan's music – from a small child to an old person, he had a musical offering for anyone who would listen.

As a young boy, Gurdas misplaced his academic and sports achievement certificates. His treasured bicycle also got stolen. He felt dejected that he had lost 'proof' of all of his life's achievements. Even though disappointed, Maan believed that this event too had a greater meaning. 'Why should I feel sad about my stolen treasures?' he reasoned aloud. 'God has His own ways. He probably took away my bicycle to bless me with a car.' His prophecy came true, as Gurdas Maan became the most loved voice of Punjab.

He rose to become the most recognisable Punjabi singer of all time, giving performances to packed audiences at prestigious venues all over the world.

"I write and sing for rights and truth, it is my duty towards Punjabi language, the beautiful entity of my country."

Gurinder Chadha

The Forthright Filmmaker / 10 Jan 1960 - Present

Once, there was a young girl called Gurinder, who lived with her family in England, and was known to ask all kinds of questions. Most of her questions would leave the adults flabbergasted and, at times, even angry.
'Mummy, why do women do all the kitchen work, while men just sit and eat?'
'Mummy, why should I wear traditional Indian clothes all the time?'
'Daddy, why should I attend a "lesser" university?'
'Teacher, why should I pursue a secretarial course and not one on developmental studies?'
Her questions were never-ending and mighty tough to answer.

Of all the questions that she used to ask, there was one that she posed to each person she met – 'Why does everyone get to have an opinion on women, except for the women themselves?' With this core question, Gurinder Chadha began her career as a filmmaker. She made a string of wonderful movies, each highlighting issues of men and women juggling multiple identities, prejudices of people, and breaking free of prejudices to live an empowered life. Pretty soon, she became a successful film director, well-known globally. Gurinder is a British-Asian woman belonging to the highly Punjabi-dominated town of Southall, married to a Japanese American man. On being asked if so many diverse influences have really been an advantage, Gurinder says with a smile, 'It will always be an advantage! It is who I am. However, the identity who I foremost am is a mother, which makes me equal to a lot of people.' To be able to choose an identity, instead of wearing the one society chooses for you, is true freedom.

The little Gurinder, who never stopped questioning social disparity and patriarchy, continues to question society through her magical, thought-provoking films. Gurinder Chadha has made the world a more empowering place for its women, one movie at a time.

"I tell stories about people who the audience might think they have nothing in common with, then they emotionally connect with them and find they're not different at all."

Harita Kaur Deol

The Woman with Wings / 10 Nov 1971 - 24 Dec 1996

This is a story of a young girl from Chandigarh named Harita. Her father wanted her to study statistics at the prestigious Panjab University in Chandigarh. She, on the other hand, wanted to chase different dreams.

In those times, when women were killed in wombs, the young and exuberant Harita wanted to touch the skies. Without telling anybody the real purpose of her visit, Harita left for Dehradun for ten days. When she returned, she was jumping up and down with joy, 'I am going to join the Air Force! I am going to join the Air Force!' This barely 20-something girl was one of the first seven cadets inducted into the Air Force as Short Service Commission officers. Harita Kaur Deol went on to complete her initial training at the Air Force Academy of Dudigal, near Hyderabad.

It was two years later, on 2 September 1994, when Harita Deol flew the Avro HS-748 at a height of nearly 10,000 feet, that she created history as India's first female solo pilot in the Indian Air Force. The five-foot-two-inch girl had suddenly grown in stature. Flight Cadet Deol was immensely appreciated for her confidence, full control and excellence in flying skills. Unfortunately, Harita died in a plane crash in December 1996, along with 24 other Air Force personnel, in a village near Andhra Pradesh.

The Indian Air Force inducted its first batch of female fighter pilots in the year 2018. It is important to remember that this journey started 20 years ago – the day the amazing Harita Kaur Deol flew solo. Each time a woman flies a plane in the vast sky, it is a tribute to the first female solo pilot in the Indian Air Force, Harita Kaur Deol. Just like an airplane leaves a trail of clouds behind, Harita left a legacy for many other women to chase their dreams.

"Both my grandfathers are army men.
I am born to serve my country."

Harjit Singh Sajjan

The Defence Doyen / 6 Sept 1970 - Present

Many years ago, a little boy and his sister used to accompany their mother to a berry farm in Vancouver. Their father worked at a nearby sawmill. Little did the immigrant parents know that they were sowing seeds of dedication and diligence in their young children – Harjit Singh Sajjan and Manjeet Kaur Sajjan.

When the young Harjit turned 20, he joined the British Columbia Regiment, and worked hard to rise to the rank of lieutenant-colonel. Life in the army took Sajjan overseas four times in his career – once to Bosnia and thrice to Afghanistan. Each posting was shaping him for a much bigger role. At one time, he had to decide to forgo his Sikh identity since the military gas masks were not compatible with the beard. To stand up for one's ideals, one does not necessarily need to fight with swords and guns. In today's times, it is possible through innovation and collaboration. So Sajjan thought, 'Can I create a mask for bearded soldiers like myself?' and he did! The mask was patented in his name as a military Sikh gas mask. He often said, 'Anyone in a leadership role needs to know that when you are looking at conflict, you can't look inward. You need to work with society.'

Harjit Sajjan also went on to become the first Sikh to command an army regiment in Canada. After having won many prestigious awards and medals for his service, the defence doyen began working as a detective with Vancouver Police Department. Just like he fought against the Taliban in Afghanistan as a military officer, he fought against drug traffickers in Vancouver as a police officer. Later, he decided to serve the people of the country through national politics. The decorated veteran went on to become the Defence Minister of Canada, making two countries proud!

"I found the true meaning of Sikhism and I loved the warrior aspect of it. When I was fighting to understand who I am, that (warrior) aspect was something that I really identified with."

Harnaam Kaur

The Bearded Beauty / 29 Nov 1990 - Present

A young girl called Harnaam Kaur stood staring at herself in the mirror. With a horrified expression, she continued to glare at the strands of hair on her face!

'Is that beard growing on my face?' she wondered in dismay. Harnaam would use her hands to hide her face while talking to her friends in school. However, the strands of hair began getting longer and thicker, till it became difficult to conceal them with the hands of an 11-year-old. Her schoolmates began bullying her and calling her names like 'Beardo' and 'She-man'.

She would often wonder why this was happening to her. Harnaam went to a doctor and found out that she suffered from a medical condition called polycystic ovary syndrome. This syndrome meant that she had more testosterone than women usually have, which led to greater hair growth all over her body.

Every day Harnaam would look at her face and try different things to rid herself of the hair. Shaving, bleaching, waxing – she tried it all! But the hair kept growing back, until one day Harnaam decided to embrace and love herself the way she was. When you love yourself, magic happens, and people begin to love you too. That is what happened with Harnaam.

She began working as a primary school teacher. People would reach out to her and tell her that they loved her beard. Harnaam Kaur became a source of inspiration for men and women to accept and love themselves. Besides teaching, Harnaam Kaur is a life coach and motivational speaker. She does get stared at every single day, but the amazing Harnaam has learnt to accept that she's different, and that is her superpower!

"I honestly think self-love is so powerful that it could stop war."

NDP

Jagmeet Singh

The Leader à la Mode / 2 Jan 1979 - Present

Jimmy was born to his immigrant parents in Ontario, Canada. His great grandfather was a revolutionary, who had fought against British occupation in India. Little Jimmy probably inherited his great-grandfather's fighting spirit, when he decided to grow up and become a criminal lawyer.

Little Jimmy's journey to becoming the self-assured, enigmatic Jagmeet Singh wasn't easy. While growing up, he often felt alone, unworthy and ashamed. He learnt to overcome adversity, and feelings of not belonging, through powerful, and sometimes traumatic lessons. As a lawyer, Jagmeet would provide free legal seminars to people in need of justice. However, he realised that in order to help more people, he would require a bigger platform. This marked the foray of Jagmeet Singh into the world of politics. He is the national leader of the New Democratic Party in Canada today.

Singh can be spotted from afar, wearing his characteristic *dumaala*, matched with stylish suits, cycling all over the streets of Canada, campaigning for issues close to his heart. He strongly feels that even though human beings may look different from each other, may pray to different gods, may eat different kinds of food and listen to different kinds of music, there is far more that unites them than divides them, such as the same need of love, support, family, education and opportunities. To a heckler who shouted at him at a public rally, the amazing Jagmeet Singh, in his signature poised demeanour, said, 'We welcome you. We support you. We believe in your rights,' and ended up winning hearts with his message of love.

"Sikhs are considered the champions of fairness, uplifting people, protecting and defending human rights. So, when someone sees a Sikh, the turban identifies a person who's going to stand up for rights, even if you disagree with them."

MISSING
MISSING

Jaswant Singh Khalra

The Immortal Illuminant / 2 Nov 1952 - 6 Sep 1995

Once, there was a brave man called Jaswant Singh Khalra, who sought to find light when his beloved state of Punjab had plunged deep into darkness. In the late 1980s, when Punjab was battling insurgency, two of Jaswant's colleagues were abducted from work. When no help came from the police, Bhai Jaswant Singh Khalra decided to set on the journey of finding his friends himself.

The journey was not easy. It led Bhai Jaswant Singh to thousands of murdered and illegally cremated Sikhs. Without fearing for his own life, he continued to bring to light the extra-judicial killings of thousands of innocent Sikhs. A lawyer by profession, he fought for human rights, and swore to bring the culprits to justice.

His research on the 25,000 illegal killings in Punjab garnered global attention. He increasingly became a threat to the system that had sanctioned the extra-judicial killings. The path that Jaswant Singh trod was a dangerous one because he had chosen to fight the police and the government. Speaking to a packed audience in Canada, his voice boomed:

"I challenge the Darkness.
If nothing else, then at least around myself I will not let it settle.
Around myself, I will establish Light.
When today, Darkness is trying to overwhelm the Truth
with full strength, then if nothing else,
self-respecting Punjab (Ankhila Punjab),
like a Lamp, is challenging this Darkness."

One September morning, Bhai Jaswant Singh was picked from outside his house to never return. It has been 26 years since his unfortunate killing. His life has given us an important lesson that challenging darkness is never easy. For that, one has to become a beacon of inextinguishable light, just like Jaswant Singh Khalra became, for the people of his *Ankhila* Punjab.

Lilly Singh

The Hard Hustler / 26 Sept 1988 - Present

The daughter of Punjabi immigrant parents, Lilly was born and raised in Canada. In her growing-up years, she saw her parents working multiple jobs to give her sister, Tina, and her, a comfortable childhood. Lilly grew up in this culture of 'hustle hard'.

When Lilly grew up, she began studying psychology in college. Life seemed to be going in a very linear fashion for her. 'Graduation, job and then marriage...,' was a voice she often heard in her head. 'Marriage cannot be the optimal achievement of my life!' revolted another voice. There was something amiss. She felt sad most of the time. One day, Lilly decided that she was going to make herself happy, and began making videos on YouTube. Slowly and gradually, people began to notice her talent, and her voice began to resonate with several young girls and boys. In the midst of her studies, she decided to take a break and make more videos because it genuinely made her happy.

'We don't understand what YouTube and making videos is, Lilly! But you take a year. If it doesn't go well, you must finish your education and find a stable job,' Lilly's parents voiced their concern. This was the beginning of a countdown for Lilly. She had one year to make more and more content for her fans. She taught herself the nuances of video-making and how to thrive in the digital world. Slowly, her hard work began to pay off. Soon, she became one of the most popular YouTube stars!

Since then, there has been no looking back for Lilly. She is now the host of a prestigious late-night show called **A Little Late with Lilly Singh**. She is also a bestselling author and a supremely popular YouTuber. Her book, **How to Be a Bawse: A Guide to Conquering Life**, reached the *New York Times* bestseller list after its release in 2017. The amazing Lilly Singh continues to hustle hard and shatter glass ceilings wherever she goes!

"Think of discomfort as currency - it's the price you pay to learn some pretty crucial things."

Maharani Jind Kaur

The Iron Lady of Punjab / 1817 - 1 Aug 1863

A long time ago, when the king, Maharaja Ranjit Singh died, it came upon his beautiful queen, Maharani Jindan (Jind Kaur), to take care of their son, Duleep Singh. She was also appointed to look after the state of Punjab, as their only son was too young then.

The British rulers thought that it would be easy to snatch their kingdom since Duleep was only a little boy, and Jindan was alone and helpless. This was their folly. They had underestimated the strong, fierce queen that Jind Kaur was. As a regent, Maharani Jindan emerged as a successful strategist, who strengthened the ties between the administration and the army. She even convinced the Governor of Hazara to pay her army more. These were the mark of not just a good leader but a strong woman as well. She forwent her veil, directly addressed her troops, and shunned practices that pulled women down.

When the British declared war with the Sikhs, Jind Kaur sent her troops to fight them. The Sikhs lost the war. Jind Kaur's powers as a regent were snatched, and her son was sent to England. She was dragged by her hair and imprisoned in a fort. However, the iron lady disguised herself and escaped to Nepal. She left a note for the British saying, 'You put me in the cage and locked me up. For all your locks and your sentries, I got out by my magic!' The British were left perplexed.

Several years later, she was reunited with her son, who had embraced Christianity as a child. During her brief stay with Duleep, Jind Kaur rekindled his love for his country and Sikhism. He returned to his faith. Just before dying, the frail but formidable Maharani Jindan had made the last Prince of Punjab remember who he was.

***"I am Rani Jindan. Mother of the Khalsa.
That is my identity. That is my fate."
– The Last Queen, Chitra Banerjee Divakaruni***

Mata Bhag Kaur

The Sikh Joan of Arc / 1666 - Mid 1700s

Many, many years ago a little girl was born to Bhai Mallo Shah in the Jhabal Kalan village in Amritsar district. Blessed with twinkling eyes and a luminous face, her parents named her Bhag, meaning the fortunate one.

Little Bhag Kaur was brought up with strong Sikh ideals and values. She grew up on stories of valour of Guru Hargobind and the martyrdom of Guru Arjun Dev, both under whom her grandfather had served. She herself wanted to be a Sikh soldier in Guru Gobind Singh's army. However, she was told that being a girl, she could not go to the battlefield. This did not stop Bhag Kaur from training in the art of warfare and horse riding, though.

The attack on Anandpur Sahib in the year 1705 changed Bhag Kaur's life forever. 40 Sikhs had deserted Guru Gobind Singh and had returned home. Angry at their betrayal, Bhag Kaur admonished them and made them realise their grave mistake. 'You deserted the Guru when He needed you the most! Shameful! I will go and fight along with Guru Gobind Singh,' she thundered.

That day saw the great metamorphosis of Bhag Kaur to the fierce *Maaee* Bhago, as she led the 40 Sikhs to the Guru, who was then stationed in Muktsar in Punjab. Before they could reach the Guru, the Mughal forces intercepted them. *Maaee* Bhago, along with the 40 Sikhs, bravely fought them. Bhag Kaur, with a small turban, called the *keski*, around her head, and a sword in her hand, created history by becoming the first woman in Punjab to have fought in a battlefield! She was the sole survivor in the Battle of Muktsar.

After the battle, Guru Gobind Singh, who had been raining arrows from the mound, came down to the battlefield and forgave the forty deserters, who were then blessed and cremated as martyrs, thanks to the valiant *Maaee* Bhago. The amazing *Maaee* Bhago joined Guru Gobind Singh and continued to serve him as a saint-soldier for the remainder of her life.

"Before you attack my Guru, come and fight me!"

Manmohan Singh

The Expert Economist / 26 Sept 1932 - Present

Once there was a little boy who moved from Gah in Pakistan to Amritsar in India, with his grandmother, after the partition in 1947. His name was Manmohan Singh. He loved to read and write. In fact, Manmohan enjoyed studying so much that he always managed to get the first position in the class.

After finishing studies in college, Manmohan was called by his professor, 'You must think big and endeavour to learn more. Why don't you go abroad and study further?' and so he did. He went on to study Economics Tripos at the University of Cambridge in England. All through his years of studying, Manmohan wanted to become a teacher. So, when he came back to India, he began teaching at a university. Several years passed. Manmohan Singh's life was all about books. The more he studied, the more he taught.

Dr Manmohan Singh became popular because of his intellectual capabilities. He was soon offered a position with the Government of India. It was a matter of few years before he became the first Sikh Prime Minister of India! A sky-blue-turbaned, bespectacled, mild-mannered Sardar changed the face of India with his revolutionary economic policies.

On being asked how a great teacher became a great world leader, Dr Manmohan Singh said, 'I was taught by great teachers myself and that is how anyone can become great at anything they want!'

"In matters of the state, one has to be full of sentiments, but one can never be sentimental."

Mata Khivi

The Langar Launcher / 1506 - 1582

A village near Khadoor Sahib in Punjab was home to a young girl, Khivi. As was the custom in those times, she was 13 when she was married off to a boy in her village called Lehna. He later became the second Guru of the Sikhs, Guru Angad Dev.

Guru Angad Dev would often address people, more specifically women, and spread the teachings of Guru Nanak. He wanted to spread the message of equality between men and women. His wife, respectfully called Mata Khivi, would keep the traditions of Guru Nanak alive in her own way. That tradition was of preparing and serving hot meals to everyone. It was under Mata Khivi's administration that this ritual of preparing and serving food among everyone became popular as ***langar***. She would take special care for ensuring these meals and eventually made this practice official. While advocating for sewa or selfless service, she would spread the idea of langar: 'Food belongs to God. It is for everyone. No single person owns it.'

In those times when women would not step out of their homes, Mata Khivi was the face of progression and modernity. She worked outside the home to establish the langar system and took care of her family as well. This is the legacy of the amazing Khivi ji, whose tradition of langar remains alive in all gurudwaras around the world.

ਲੰਗਰੁ ਚਲੈ ਗੁਰ ਸਬਦਿ ਹਰਿ ਤੋਟਿ ਨ ਆਵੀ ਖਟੀਐ ॥

Langar Chalai Gur Shabad Har Tott Na Aavai Khatteeai.

"The Langar - the Kitchen of the Guru's Shabad has been opened, and its supplies never run short."
—(Ang 967 in Guru Granth Sahib)

Mohinder Singh Randhawa

The Outstanding Officer / 2 Feb 1909 - 3 Mar 1986

A long time ago, a young schoolboy from Shri Muktsar Sahib in Punjab, called Mohinder, would address himself as 'Dr M.S. Randhawa'. He would even post a letter from the Governor of Punjab to himself, with the prefix 'Dr' to his name! When his flabbergasted father would question him about it, the young boy would confidently say that such a letter would arrive one day.

The hard-working Mohinder Singh Randhawa cleared the Indian Civil Service (ICS) exam in the first attempt and went on to serve as deputy commissioner. Randhawa was the Deputy Commissioner of Delhi on the eve of India's independence. He was responsible for the smooth execution of the function wherein Pandit Jawaharlal Nehru would deliver his historic 'Tryst with destiny' speech. Dr Randhawa practised the unfurling of the Indian flag every hour to ensure a well-ordered function. Such was his perfectionism!

Mohinder Randhawa wore many a hat. He was a prolific writer who penned several books on history, art, and culture. His love for trees and gardens was well known. He even earned a doctorate in science for his work on algae. He gave Chandigarh, the capital city of Punjab, the gift of the iconic Rose Garden. The man behind the establishment of the Punjab Agricultural University in Ludhiana and the Government Museum and Art Gallery in Chandigarh was none other than Dr M.S. Randhawa.

Le Corbusier designed Chandigarh; however, Dr M.S. Randhawa gave the city its soul. He said that Chandigarh could not just be a bureaucratic hostel; it needed to be beautified. 'The people of this city will have largesse like the trees, and the trees of this city will have a persona like humans,' he prophesied. The city of Chandigarh is breathtakingly beautiful in spring, and Dr M.S. Randhawa continues to breathe through the blooming Amaltas trees that are lined across the streets of the city.

"Punjab, besides its agriculture and industry, needs to save and cherish its rich art and culture. Only if we can save our language, will we be able to save our identity."

Narinder Singh Kapany

Unsung Father of Fibre Optics / 31 Oct 1926 - 4 Dec 2020

Narinder's story begins in the dusty town of Punjab called Moga. This young boy went on to study at the Agra University. He served in India for a while and then left for Imperial College in London in 1952 to pursue a doctorate in optics. After that, there was no looking back for Dr Narinder Singh Kapany.

Kapany, along with his guide Harold Hopkins, worked on transmission through fibres. He made a path-breaking discovery that images could be transmitted over a bundle of optic fibres. In fact, it was Dr Kapany who later coined the term 'fibre optics'. His research led to great things in the digital revolution, such as high-speed broadband, internet, laser technology for surgeries, and so on. However, Professor Charles K. Kao, who began work in the same field as Kapany many years later, won a Nobel Prize in the field of optics in 2009. The scientific community was left shocked because of Kapany's exclusion from the coveted recognition. Nevertheless, Narinder Kapany himself was least disturbed about it. 'I don't think there should be any controversy about it. It is up to the Swedish Academy to decide. They have used whatever criteria they wanted to use,' he said magnanimously. Although Dr Kapany did not get the recognition that was due, he did not allow this event to discourage him from working towards his dreams. This is what sets amazing people apart from others – they always see the bigger picture. He went on to establish his own companies called Optics Technology Inc. and K2 Optronics in Silicon Valley. Besides being a successful entrepreneur, Dr Kapany taught and supervised students for years at prestigious universities.

This trailblazer Sikh from Moga had one idea – 'light need not travel in a straight line' – which he carried with him all the way to college. Look how far it took him!

"I was just a precocious kid taking a college physics course when one day the professor told us that light always travels in a straight line. But that can't be true, I thought, it must be bent sometimes!"

Navjot Singh Sidhu

Statesman in the Making / 20 Oct 1963 - Present

Once upon a time, in the princely town of Patiala in Punjab, lived a lanky teenager called Navjot Singh. As a teenager, his father, Bhagwant Singh Sidhu, would force the lanky boy out of bed every single day, in the wee hours of the morning, and send him for practice. He dreamt that his son would play cricket for the country one day.

Navjot could not defy his disciplinarian father. In due course, his hard work started paying off. He made his debut by playing for Punjab against Services in Amritsar. However, after that, a string of dismal performances followed. He began to be written off in the newspapers. One of the articles even called him 'a stroke-less wonder'. This particular newspaper article left a deep impact on him. Navjot decided it was time to take his cricketing career seriously. He pasted this scathing article on his mirror. Each morning, he would wake up and vow to turn the tide. Come rain, come shine, Navjot practised religiously every day.

Gradually, Navjot Singh Sidhu matured to emerge as a commendable cricketer, creating a record of sorts with over 500 test runs in a year, thrice! Another article was written by the same journalist, wherein he was rechristened – ***From a Stroke-less Wonder to A Palm-Hitting Grove***. 'That day, I cried and cried. I had finally realised my father's dream!' he recalled.

This was followed by a marathon of fulfilling many more dreams, like becoming a famous commentator for cricket matches and entering politics and winning party elections. However, one of his special achievements has been to help open a road corridor between India and Pakistan, which enabled Indians to visit Gurudwara Darbar Sahib Kartarpur, one of the holiest sites for the Sikhs. The eventful journey might not have been easy for Navjot, but this feisty Sardar has shown to the world that dedication, focus and perseverance can do wonders in life.

"A revolutionary idea is usually one with its sleeves rolled up."

Partap Singh Kairon

Architect of Modern Punjab / 1 Oct 1901 - 6 Feb 1965

This is a story of a young boy Partap, who went for his further studies to the United States of America. While studying political science and economics, he also worked in factories and farms to support himself. Impressed with modern farming in the US, he would often say to himself, 'Once I return to India, I will replicate these farming methods in my own country.'

However, on returning to India, Partap got actively involved in politics. He held several offices, the most prominent being his role as the rehabilitation minister and development minister. The Partition between India and Pakistan had left millions of people homeless and jobless. Kairon re-established the refugees with new homes and created job opportunities for them. Later, as the Chief Minister of Punjab, he worked for the state and remembered his resolve years ago – to bring prosperity from farms in the US to farms in Punjab. Therefore, Partap worked to lay down the foundation for Green Revolution in Punjab, encouraged big industries to set up in the state, and consolidated small land holdings. Stellar institutions such as **Punjab Agricultural University (PAU)** were the brainchild of Partap Singh Kairon – the quintessential farmer at heart. He even set up the **Postgraduate Institute of Medical Education (PGIMER)**, **Kurukshetra University** and **Punjabi University**.

During the Indo-China war in 1962, he told the people of Punjab,

"Remember our Sikh Gurus, and their crusade to fight for the righteous cause. You too, come forward, and join the nation in our fight against the enemy!"

Partap Singh Kairon's words created great stir and fervour among the people of Punjab as they contributed nearly 130 kgs of gold towards the national war effort! Nearly 55 years after his death, the amazing Partap Singh Kairon lives on in the progressive and enduring institutions he built – truly the architect of modern Punjab.

Puran Singh

The Quixotic Mystic / 17 Feb 1881 - 31 Mar 1931

Long time ago, a boy called Puran Singh, lived in Abbottabad, a city now in Pakistan. He was exceptionally good in his studies and even got a scholarship to study biochemistry from the Tokyo University in Japan. While studying in Japan, Puran came in contact with several Buddhist monks, and he embraced Buddhism and shaved his head to become a monk himself. Later, *Bhikshu* Puran, as he began to be popularly called, met a famous teacher of Hindu philosophy, Swami Ram Tirath, and chose to become a *swami* himself. Puran now became *Swami* Puran and began wearing orange clothes like his teacher.

After finishing his studies, Puran came back to India, and began working as a forest chemist in Dehradun. He was invited to the Sikh Educational Conference in 1912, to give a talk on agriculture. It was at this conference that Puran met the great saint-poet, Bhai Vir Singh. They talked endlessly about spirituality, faith and life. Their conversations made Swami Puran want to return to Sikhism. He followed his heart yet again, and came back to his roots, culture and literature with greater vigour and clarity.

Professor Puran Singh went on to write several books and poems in English and Punjabi languages. He paid homage to the Sikh scriptures by translating them into English and making them accessible to the world. Before succumbing to tuberculosis, Professor Puran Singh wrote three volumes of the classic, **Spirit of the Sikh**. From *Bhikhshu* Puran to *Swami* Puran, and finally to Professor Puran Singh, this journey of the revolutionary Punjabi poet, scientist and mystic was nothing short of a miracle.

The path of spirituality may be long and difficult. One may flounder and get lost every once in a while, but the secret is to never give up on finding the final destination.

"Love is the simple, inmost state of life which depends on no outward conditions of life. As the seed is to the pine-tree, love is to the true man."

Parkash Kaur

Mother Hope / Unknown - Present

Once upon a time, there was a small girl who would grow up and save many other girls like her, but she almost got killed herself. She was abandoned in a drain a few hours after her birth. She cried and cried till someone heard her wails and came and rescued her. When she grew up, she decided to dedicate her life to rescuing unwanted children. 'I will create a home, where babies like me can be loved and cherished,' Parkash Kaur promised herself.

At the young age of 24, Parkash Kaur started an orphanage for girls called **'Unique Home'** in the city of Jalandhar in Punjab. She rescued several baby girls who were abandoned in drains, some wrapped in plastic bags and blankets, and some even left in a cradle outside her home. She looked after them, clothed and fed them, and gave them a safe home to stay.

In Punjab, a state known for female foeticide, Parkash Kaur has rescued 60 abandoned girls, who all call her mother. She provides them with education and a secure future. It was not easy to run the orphanage, but gradually, people got to know about her noble venture. They began donating grocery items, clothes and books for abandoned baby girls. 'God always finds a way to provide for us,' she says with a smile.

This is what happens to good deeds. They create a ripple effect – one good deed leads to another and another. 60 years ago, someone rescued little Parkash Kaur, and today she continues to save disowned and deserted children and lights up their lives.

"My Guru has bestowed on me this duty to give love and care to little baby girls who unfortunately didn't receive the love they deserved."

Bhai Ram Singh

The Royal Architect / 4 Jun 1904 - 5 Aug 1992

Ram Singh was a carpenter's son. He came from a small village called Rasul, in Gurdaspur, Punjab. As a young boy, he would intently watch his father at work. He would also accompany his father to the wood-carver's shop, where he worked on daily wages.

Real talent always shines through regardless of where one is in life. The young Ram Singh was picked up from that wood-carver's shop one day, to pursue the study of arts and craft at the reputable Mayo School of Arts in Lahore, which is now called the National College of Arts.

That was the turning point in Singh's life. Ram's wood carving left Queen Victoria so impressed that she invited him to England in the year 1891 to design the **Darbar Hall** in her palace. His craftsmanship was recognised and duly awarded by honouring Ram Singh with the Order of British Empire (OBE). On returning from Britain, Ram Singh took a position as the Principal of Mayo School of Arts in Lahore. In a letter that he wrote regarding his promotion to the then lieutenant governor of Punjab, he mentioned among many other accomplishments his first job and skilled craftsmanship even as an untrained 14-year-old. 'I repaired and polished Lady Young's piano, and my work was approved even then...,' he humbly wrote.

Ram Singh also worked as an independent architect. He designed the **Senate Hall** at the Punjab University, **Forman Christian College**, **Lahore Museum**, **Mayo School of Arts in Lahore**, and the historically identical, Indo-Saracenic style buildings of **Khalsa College, Amritsar** and **Aitchison College in Lahore**.

Bhai Ram Singh is the pioneer of Sikh architecture. Hailing from a family of carpenters, he inherited an innate sense of design. Every single day, when Ram Singh would work at the wood carver's shop, who knew he was unknowingly chiselling his own future and creating history!

"Architecture should speak of its time and place, but yearn for timelessness." – (Frank Gehry)

Maharaja Ranjit Singh

The Lion of Punjab / 13 Nov 1780 - 7 Jun 1839

Ranjit Singh, the powerful king, ruled far and wide – from Kashmir in the north to deserts of Sindh in the south, from Khyber Pass in the west to the river Sutlej in the east. He was like no other king. Having lost sight of his left eye during childhood to smallpox, Ranjit Singh didn't look quite elegant. Moreover, he had a weather-beaten complexion and a short height. However, he was one of the finest soldiers with the kindest heart that the world would see. It has been famously said that no other king, except the great Maharaja Ranjit Singh, has ever created an empire as big with criminality as little. No matter what the world has us believe, Maharaja Ranjit Singh showed that one could be powerful without hurting others.

Although bestowed with imposing titles, Ranjit Singh preferred to be addressed as Singh Sahib. Unlike autocratic leaders, who enjoy flattery and flamboyance, Ranjit Singh did not wear any special emblems of royalty or create government seals and coins in his name. Only occasionally, the Maharaja would wear the *Koh-I-Noor* diamond on his arm. 'In my empire, Sikhs, Muslims and Hindus will enjoy equal opportunities and rights,' Maharaja Ranjit Singh would firmly say. His liberal thoughts reflected in his council of ministers, who came from all walks of life. His Muslim and Hindu wives continued to practice their own faiths.

Maharaja Ranjit Singh came to be known as the '***Lion of Punjab***', and he truly lived up to his name, Ranjit – Victor in Battle. He was a master strategist, who along with his closest collaborators, his mother-in-law, Sada Kaur, the army chief, Fateh Singh Ahluvalia, and later the fierce soldier, Akali Phula Singh, managed to bring entire Punjab under his control. After taking Amritsar under his reign, people also witnessed the spiritual side of the Maharaja. A devout Sikh, Ranjit Singh, would visit the Golden Temple frequently. The gold canopy offered by him is preserved to date.

"The land of Gurus and saints will now be ruled by Punjabis, where there will be no discrimination based on religion or creed."

Rupi Kaur

The Poet Who Paints Parables / 4 Oct 1992 - Present

Her father used to regale little Rupi Kaur with stories every night. He would especially tell her wonderful stories about the poet-warrior, Guru Gobind Singh. Inspired by tales on Sikh culture, Rupi began writing. She wrote anonymously on issues close to her heart.

Gradually, Rupi Kaur gathered the courage to add her name to her work. Her short and thought-provoking poems began to resonate with people around the world. She even began to add simple illustrations to her poems. Her poems were powerful because they carried ideas that were important. A collection of her poems was published as her first book, **milk and honey**, in the year 2014. Rupi Kaur's maiden book sold more than 2.5 million copies, and was also translated into 25 languages. Her second book, **the sun and her flowers**, published in 2017, garnered the young poet a lot of praise from all quarters.

Rupi writes about feminity, love, self-care, abuse, and heartbreak. A #1 *New York Times* bestseller author, Kaur prefers to write in small case – a concept inspired from Gurmukhi script. 'I love that all letters in Gurmukhi are treated the same,' she says.

"as a father of three daughters
it would have been normal
for him to push marriage on us
this has been the narrative for
the women in my culture for hundreds of years
instead he pushed education
knowing it would set us free
in a world that wanted to contain us
he made sure that we learned
to walk independently"

KHALSA AID

Ravinder Singh

The Honourable Humanitarian / 1969 - Present

Not too long ago, a little boy called Ravinder, would often play in the fields of his village Mundian Jattan in Punjab. He was 11 years old when he immigrated to West London with his family. This new life abroad was very different from the one that he had lived in India. He often wondered how far he had drifted from home, his language and his culture!

Ravinder Singh, on moving to the UK, gave up his identity as a Sikh. He shaved off his beard and stopped tying the turban. It took an encounter with a well-meaning friend to rekindle his lost faith. When Ravi embraced Sikhism once again, he did it wholeheartedly. After all, Sikhism is not just about tying a turban and sporting a beard. It is about understanding and following its principles of *sarbat da bhala* – well-being for all. He made this the motto of his life and launched **Khalsa Aid**, an organisation that would work towards the well-being of all humanity. 'We need to go beyond faith and humanity. You can learn a lot by being human,' he told everyone.

It was the beginning of a series of selfless deeds – deeds for *sarbat da bhala*. Khalsa Aid became synonymous with well-intentioned Sikh men and women who worked overtime, feeding and providing rescue and relief to victims of disasters all over the world. Be it earthquakes in Haiti, a tsunami in the Andamans, Islamic State (IS) persecutions in Syria, Boko Haram wars in Nigeria, Ravinder Singh and his soldiers of Khalsa Aid expeditiously delivered aid to people in distress. The Khalsa Aid is now a large organisation, with volunteers belonging to different races, colours and creeds. However, the message Ravinder Singh endorses – blessings for all – is what binds them all to the common thread of humanity.

No matter how disillusioned one gets, a good friend or family member can help one to rediscover one's faith and principles, just like it happened with Ravi Singh. This rediscovery put him on a much higher path of spirituality for times to come, making him a beacon of hope and peace for people globally.

"Drop food, not bombs."

Sada Kaur

The Diplomatic Warrior / 1762 - 1832

Once upon a time, there was a young woman called Rani Sada Kaur who lost her husband at an early age, fighting in the Battle of Batala. The now-widowed Sada Kaur had a little daughter to take care of. Life offered her two tough options – either she could lead the rest of her life at the mercy of others or lift herself and rise above her circumstances. The brave woman that she was, she chose the latter. This decision became the turning point of her life.

One of the first things that Sada Kaur did was to adorn herself with a turban, armour, and weaponry. She assumed the leadership of Kanhaiya Misl, which was one of the sovereign states of the Sikh confederacy and began to command battles, thus laying the foundation for the Sikh empire. The second turning point in Sada Kaur's life came when she married her daughter, Mehtab Kaur, to Maharaja Ranjit Singh. Thereafter, Sada Kaur became the Maharaja's advisor and guide, as he took over as emperor of the new Sikh empire.

When Ranjit Singh was approached by citizens of Lahore to put an end to Bhangi Misl's misrule, he sought advice from his visionary mother-in-law. Mata Sada Kaur said, 'Son, whoever controls Lahore, will also become the master of Punjab. Go and conquer Lahore, but do not plunder and inflict suffering on innocent citizens!' She spread the word that Ranjit Singh and his army were heading to Amritsar, and told them to reach Lahore instead, in the middle of the night. Upon reaching Lahore, Ranjit Singh's army fell short, as they didn't have cannons to fight and capture the fort. Sada Kaur managed to convince their opponent, Chaet Singh, to hand over the fort peacefully, lest there be bloodshed as Ranjit Singh had come armed with heavy cannons! Chaet Singh agreed, and Ranjit Singh captured Lahore without any plundering. In this way, the brilliant warrior-strategist Sada Kaur helped Ranjit Singh to become the formidable Maharaja of the Sikh Empire, thus writing an illustrious chapter in history.

"So long as the Maharaja is the sovereign of his own kingdom, it is the same as if I am the sovereign."

Sham Singh Attariwala

The Glorious General / 1790 - 10 Feb 1846

A son was born to Sardar Nihal Singh of Attari village, located just a few kilometres from the India-Pakistan border. He was named Sham Singh. This little boy grew up to lead the army of Maharaja Ranjit Singh. As the sun set on the Maharaja's grand empire, the world stood witness to the valour and bravery of the glorious general, Sham Singh Attariwala.

The army was facing huge losses during the first Anglo-Sikh war, also called the Battle of Sabhrawan. Sham Singh, who was nearly 60-years-old by then, was called to join the battle. Two of the other generals, Lal Singh and Tej Singh, deserted Sham Singh Attariwala, thus leaving him alone in a dangerous situation. However, this did not crush the spirit of the valiant general. He considered himself to be a true disciple of Guru Gobind Singh. Sham Singh pledged to die in the battle rather than return in defeat.

He led the army, dressed in white silks, and charged towards the opponents on his white stallion. The grey-bearded saint-soldier led his army of Khalsa soldiers and fought courageously against the British till his last breath. He was overpowered and fell to the ground.

Unfortunately, his death marked the end of the great Sikh empire. For the valiant Sham Singh Attariwala, it was never about merely winning or losing. He knew that a true hero is one who knows that it is always about not quitting.

ਸੂਰਾ ਸੋ ਪਹਿਚਾਨੀਐ ਜੁ ਲਰੈ ਦੀਨ ਕੇ ਹੇਤ ॥
ਪੁਰਜਾ ਪੁਰਜਾ ਕਟਿ ਮਰੈ ਕਬਹੂ ਨ ਛਾਡੈ ਖੇਤੁ ॥

Soora So Pehchaniyai Jo Larey Deen Ke Hayt.
Purja Purja Kat Marai Kabhoo Na Chhaadai Khet.

"He alone is known as a spiritual hero, who fights in defense of religion. He may be cut apart, piece by piece, but he never leaves the field of battle."
—(Ang 1105, Guru Granth Sahib)

Sobha Singh

The Prolific Painter / 29 Nov 1901 - 22 Aug 1986

Sobha Singh, a young man from Gurdaspur in Punjab, was born to a Sikh family; his father served in the Indian cavalry. In 1919, he got recruited into the British Indian Army to make technical drawings and plans. This job as a draughtsman took him to Baghdad, Mesopotamia, which is now Iraq. After a few years of service, Sobha left the army and returned to Amritsar – the city where he had studied art and craft for one year. He opened his art studio in Amritsar in 1923 and thereafter moved to the then-cultural hub of undivided India, Lahore. However, this wasn't for too long. Sobha wanted to live in a place that was as serene as his paintings. So, after the partition of India, he permanently shifted to Andretta village in Kangra, Himachal Pradesh, a picturesque hamlet on the foothills of the mighty Himalayas.

He stayed in Andretta with his family for 38 long years. Nestled in beautiful surroundings, away from the hustle-bustle of city life, Sobha Singh painted happily and in peace. He played with colours on canvas and gave life to his paintings. The talented artist created several masterpieces, out of which the most well-known paintings have been those of Guru Nanak and Guru Gobind Singh. Sobha Singh's paintings of the Gurus display infinite peace and tranquillity. They are also rich and descriptive. He has also been credited for lending a face to *Sohni-Mahiwal*, the popular tragic romance of Punjab. However, the focus of his paintings remained the Sikh Gurus. 'I have painted the Gurus to inspire people,' he would say.

Sobha's super power was to give a face to characters which one can only feel in one's heart. Most of the Sikh households are incomplete without the divine paintings of the Gurus, and almost always, each carries his trademark signature. He truly was the 'Painter of the People'.

"A painting is complete when it has the shadows of God." – (Rembrandt)

Sohan Singh Bhakna

The Ghadri Hero / 22 Jan 1870 - 21 Dec 1968

Among the many illustrious Sikh portraits installed in the Central Sikh Museum in the Golden Temple at Amritsar, there stands tall a portrait of an unassuming, gentle-looking Sardar with a flowing beard. This man had laid the foundation of a revolutionary party of its times – the Ghadar Party.

Born and raised in a small village in Amritsar, Sohan Singh became active in the early nationalist movement in India in the 1900s. He decided to move out of Punjab because of economic depression and agrarian unrest. A two-month-long and difficult journey took him to Seattle in the United States. Sohan found work in a timber mill, where he met many immigrants.

Over time, Sohan realised that the entire community was facing racism and discrimination. Sensing injustice, Bhakna decided to formalise the community's struggle by laying the foundation of the Ghadar Party. The party was headquartered in San Francisco. Their main goal was to overthrow the British Empire. The Komagata Maru incident, wherein a group of people from British India were denied entry to Canada, and the ship was forced to return to Calcutta, further strengthened their resolve to fight against discrimination. Bhakna began organising the Ghadar Conspiracy to direct their collective rebellion against the oppressive regime. However, before his plans could materialise, British intelligence arrested Sohan Singh Bhakna and sentenced him to life imprisonment in the Andaman Islands.

He would often say, 'I am neither a Leninist nor a Gandhian; my only dream was Indian independence and prosperity of Indian people.' The fight of a true revolutionary does not die behind bars. Its flame keeps burning bright. Sohan Singh continued to carry out hunger strikes in jail, fought for Sikh prisoners' religious rights, and campaigned for Bhagat Singh. Sohan Singh Bhakna lived to the ripe age of 98, and his campaign for justice and equality lives on forever.

"No man is worth his salt who is not ready at all times to risk his body, to risk his well-being, to risk his life in great cause." – (Theodore Roosevelt)

VOTE FOR WOMEN
VOTE FOR WOMEN

Sophia Duleep Singh

The Suffragette Princess / 8 Aug 1876 - 22 Aug 1948

Princess Sophia was the daughter of Maharani Bamba Müller and Maharaja Duleep Singh, the last king of the Sikh empire. She lived in England. After the Maharani's untimely death, Queen Victoria took Sophia under her wing and became her godmother. Sophia lived like a true princess – breeding championship dogs, pursuing photography, and attending social gatherings.

She became quiet and withdrawn when her father passed away in 1893. Wanting to reconnect with her roots, she planned a trip to India. That journey to revisit her native land changed the course of Sophia's life forever. In India, she witnessed extreme poverty and famine, and saw the dark side of the British Empire. Chance meetings with freedom fighters languishing in jails on false cases of sedition turned her against the Empire.

She went back to England as a changed person and joined the famous Emmeline Pankhurst in her movement for women's rights. Sophia supported the movement by funding the suffragette groups and leading the cause. The erstwhile socialite now sold *The Suffragette* newspaper from outside her home! She remained a fierce voice and campaigned for women's rights defiantly. She refused to pay taxes to the British Empire. 'When the women of England are enfranchised, I shall pay my taxes willingly. If I am not a fit person for the purposes of representation, why should I be a fit person for taxation?' she protested. The movement became a success. In 1928, women over the age of 21 won the right to vote.

The last king of the Sikh Empire, Maharaja Duleep Singh, may have had to abdicate his kingdom and exile to England, but his valorous daughter, Sophia Duleep Singh, wrote history by playing an instrumental role in winning voting rights for women in Britain.

"Taxation without representation is a tyranny."

Surinder Kaur

The Nightingale of Punjab / 25 Nov 1929 - 14 Jun 2006

Hailing from a Sikh family in Lahore, as a little girl, Surinder Kaur was quite different from other girls of her age. While most of her friends would play with dolls, she was deeply drawn towards the sounds of musical instruments such as the *ghungroo* and *mankey*. She had an ear for traditional Punjabi music. The minute Surinder would hear foot-tapping music, she would be transported to a faraway land – a land where she would sing and clap with joy! Surinder's brother would watch his sister intently. He recognised her talent and passion for music, and encouraged her to learn music under Ustad Inayat Hussain.

It was in 1943 when Surinder auditioned for a radio show for children. From there on, she began to get popular. People loved to hear her sing. However, the world is full of people who will find fault even when there's none. Surinder found her share of such people too. 'Girls from good families don't sing,' they would tell her. However, Surinder's superpower was to not let the doubters stop her from following her passion. Along with her older sister, Prakash Kaur, she sang hundreds of folksongs. She later sang with Asa Singh Mastana, another legend of his times. The songs they recorded together were few, but they left an indelible mark in the world of Punjabi music. 'As long as I sang, I did so with honour and pride,' she said, rebuking her detractors.

She strongly believed that people would always listen to folk songs, also called *lokgeet*. She would say with conviction, 'All genres of music will come and go, but *lokgeet* will always remain alive.'

It has been nearly 15 years since the stunning Surinder Kaur passed away, but her songs and folklores still remain a part of Punjabi traditions and celebrations across the world. The nightingale will continue to croon till eternity, keeping the spirit of Punjabi culture alive!

"Folk songs can bring hearts together, no matter how far you live, no matter how different you may be. I love this magical power of folk music!"

Surjit Singh Patar

The Wordsmith / 14 Jan 1945 - Present

Born in a small village called Pattar Kalan, in Punjab's Jalandhar district, a young boy called Surjit, loved reading and writing from a very young age. As he grew older, he read as many books as he could lay his hands on. The more he read, the more he fell in love with literature. Surjit read throughout his entire school and college life, and after that attained a doctorate in literature from the Guru Nanak Dev University, Amritsar.

After finishing his studies, Surjit began working as a professor of Punjabi at the Punjab Agricultural University, Ludhiana. Now and then, he would scribble some words on paper. A full-time job can make it difficult to pursue one's passion. However, his hunger for letters and words never really faded. After retirement from work, Surjit Singh completely began devoting his time to writing poetry. He began writing under his pen-name 'Patar', and wrote about trees and fields and strength and hope. Surjit Patar's poems would often find a special mention of nature, more specifically, of trees. 'Why trees?' he'd be asked. 'Crops come and go, but trees age just like human beings,' the legendary poet would say in his characteristic matter-of-fact way.

The biggest superpower of the immensely popular Surjit Patar is his ability to string together words and provide hope even in the darkest of times. His magical poems are a gift of hope to people.

ਜੇ ਆਈ ਪਤਝੜ ਤਾਂ ਫੇਰ ਕੀ ਹੈ / *Je aayi pat jharh ta fer ki hai*
ਤੂ ਅਗਲੀ ਰੁੱਤ ਤੇ ਯਕੀਨ ਰੱਖੀਂ / *Tu agli rutt te yakeen rakhin*
ਮੈ ਲੱਭ ਕੇ ਲਿਆਉਨਾਂ ਕਿਤੋਂ ਕਲਮਾਂ / *Main labh ke lyona kiton kalmaa*
ਤੂੰ ਫੁੱਲਾਂ ਜੋਗੀ ਜ਼ਮੀਨ ਰੱਖੀਂ / *Tu fulaan jogi zameen rakhin*

"Do not fear the storm,
Have faith that the season will change,
I will go and find us some seeds,
You find space, enough for the flowers to blossom."

Master Tara Singh

The Stalwart Sikh / 24 Jun 1885 - 22 Nov 1967

Long ago, a young boy called Nanak Chand loved to hear stories of the sacrifices and heroism of Sikhs. The more he heard these stories, the more he began to grow fond of Sikhism. By the time Nanak Chand turned 16, he had decided to embrace the religion and subsequently changed his name to Tara Singh.

Tara Singh studied hard, and after having graduated from college, he started working as a teacher at the Khalsa High School in Lyallpur. He fondly began to be called 'Master', meaning teacher, and became popular as Master Tara Singh.

Master Tara Singh loved his faith and his job. Interestingly, Sikh politics was an intersection of his two loves. He realised that as a Sikh politician, he could follow his faith and advocate it too, and thus contribute as a teacher on a greater level. Gradually, Master Tara Singh began working for the organisation which managed gurudwaras, called the Shiromani Gurdwara Parbandhak Committee. Such was his devotion towards Sikh causes that it often led to conflict with the authorities, for which he was jailed nearly 14 times!

Master Tara Singh would raise issues such as freedom from control of gurdwaras by priests. Another burning issue he strongly protested for was a Punjabi-speaking state. Master Tara Singh began to fast unto death for this cause. 'I will not eat till we are granted a state of our own,' the short-statured, gutsy Singh declared. He broke his fast after 48 days only when the then-Prime Minister, Jawaharlal Nehru, promised to consider the issue. It was only after his assurance that Tara Singh decided to side with India after partition. Eventually, the Punjabi-speaking state, called the Punjabi *Suba*, was created. Master Tara Singh's biggest dream had come true. With a quiet smile on his lips and a sparkle in his eyes, he would say, '*Mai maraan, mera panth jeevey!*' (I may die, but my community should live on!) The panth towards which he dedicated his entire life continues to live and thrive today in all its glory.

"I dream of a vibrant, progressive Punjabi Suba, a portion of Punjab as a Sikh state."

Teja Singh Samundri

The Social Warrior / 20 Feb 1882 - 17 Jul 1926

Many years ago, there was a young boy called Teja Singh, from the Samundri *Tehsil* in the Lyallpur district of Punjab, who would read books on Sikh religion and history long after his school hours. He didn't stay in school for too long but gained real education from the books he read of the great Sikh heroes. He longed to be like them.

After working for a few years in the army, he decided to return to his village and resolved to work for the society, promoting Sikh ideals. Teja Singh believed that for religion to prevail, grassroots social issues needed to be addressed first. The stories that he had read on those long afternoons had taught him the importance of education. So, he first established 4 schools in the Amritsar and Lyallpur districts of Punjab. Then, he helped found a Sikh daily newspaper called ***Akali***. When the British Government decided to demolish one of the walls of Gurudwara Rakab Ganj in Delhi, he challenged them, saying, 'To demolish it, you will have to go over my dead body!' He was arrested for protesting against imperial repression, but did not give up.

The great social warrior became the vice-president of the SGPC, an organisation of nominated Sikh representatives for managing Sikh shrines and a leading figure of the Gurudwara Reform Movement, in which he fought fiercely to wrest control of gurudwaras from chief priests called *mahants*, and give it back to the Sikhs. In one such movement called the Guru ka Bagh Morcha, Teja Singh, along with other Sikhs, fought and won against Sundar Das, a mahant, who denied Sikhs wood from the premises of Guru ka Bagh for langar. Two years later, Teja Singh was arrested during the Jaito Morcha, wherein he had protested against the high handedness of the British government in dethroning the Maharaja of Nabha. Sadly, he suffered a heart attack while in custody at the Central Jail in Lahore, and passed away at the young age of 46. The majestic Teja Singh Samundri Hall, which is the only building dedicated to a non-Guru in the Golden Temple complex, stands tall today as a befitting tribute to this super Sikh social warrior.

"We need our own newspaper, so that we can tell the world our own stories without fear."

My Favourite Amazing Sikh!

Draw a portrait of your favourite Amazing Sikh and post it on Facebook and Instagram with the hashtag #OneAmazingSikhataTime!

Epilogue

They say art is an imitation of life. Some lives are period films, whereas others are soap operas. A few, however, are like enigmatic narratives, mysteriously woven by a binding thread over generations. Maybe ours falls into this category.

On 30 June 1930, in a village in Faridkot district, Kot Sukhia, a little boy was born into a family who owed allegiance to the Gadhri Babas. He was named Gurnam Singh. Over time, the family fell into difficulty. Their political leanings resulted in the patriarch being jailed and the land being confiscated by the British-era *munsif*. Gurnam Singh, however, had unwavering faith in the indomitable spirit of Dashmesh Pita Guru Gobind Singh. He somehow managed to get himself educated along with his four brothers and two sisters. Since childhood, he used to pen a few lines off and on. His teacher encouraged him to write and recite in the school functions. Said his teacher, 'You are a devout Sikh and inspired by Guru Gobind Singh.'

Guru Sahib was a saint-soldier and a poet. He had the most powerful expression and beautifully wove words into poetry. The teacher said, 'As his disciple, you ought to honour the talent that the Almighty has bestowed on you. Your expression is akin to precision bombardment.'

ਤੀਰ ਵਾਂਗੂ ਤਿੱਖਾ 'ਤੇ ਸਿੱਧਾ ਨਿਸ਼ਾਨੇ ਤੇ

'Tir waangu tikkha tey siddha nishaaney tey'

(Sharp and straight, like an arrow)

The words proved prophetic. 'Tir' became his synonym, and he rose to be one of the most-read humour writers of the period.

Partap Singh Kairon, the Chief Minister of the Punjab province (then comprising Haryana, Himachal, and Punjab), pestered him to come and settle in Chandigarh in 1958. Gurnam Singh was then the State Press Liaison Officer in Delhi and close to Pandit Nehru. Not keen on returning to Punjab and, wary of the experiment by the name of 'Chandigarh', he politely begged off. Kairon persisted, 'Come, this town will soon become your home, and your name will become synonymous with the place.' Prophetically again, he came in 1960 and passed away in 1991 after winning the hearts of the Punjabi diaspora, the world over as *Chacha Chandigarhia*.

As his only child, I was always in awe of him. Seerat, my firstborn, was the apple of his eye. We named her Seerat, and he chose to call her Kinnu. 'Why Kinnu of all names, Papa?' I asked.

'Just wait and watch her grow and blossom. *Kinnu* is a fruit that is both tangy and sweet, has immense health benefits, and its fragrance overpowers the stench of slush effortlessly wherever it is planted.' Prophetically again, my shy little doll discarded her Barbies and puzzles to pick up the pen and address the world on unspoken issues. Even if the content was familiar, the manner is fresh. Her sensitivity is absorbed in the pen she holds. Her hard-hitting logic makes a mark on the paper she produces. She has undertaken the task of re-introducing the young minds to the world they inherited yet might be ignorant of. 'In the era of laptops, Kindle, and Google, the art of narration is still far more important. Words have the magical power of opening a window in a stubborn brick wall,' she says.

As I said, the tale lives on...
Wishing each reader, a fulfilling experience.

Sincerely,
Bubbu Tir

Acknowledgements

If there is one thing that I've learnt over the years is that good things never happen in isolation. They are a cumulative result of the efforts of different people under different circumstances. *One Amazing Sikh at a Time* too, did not happen in a silo. When I join the dots, I see a constellation of people and events that have brought this book to life.

A big thank you to my Nani (maternal grandmother) in heaven, who was my roommate, my best friend and my first storyteller. Bedtime was incomplete without listening to Guru Sahib's Saakhiyaan. She made me fall in love with stories. This tradition of storytelling was carried on by my Daadi (paternal grandmother), who regaled my sister and me, with real-life stories of Partition, migration from her hometown Nankana Sahib (Pakistan), refugee camps, her struggles to build a life and start afresh in Nawanshehar, Punjab (India). Thank you, Nani and Daadi. What would childhood have been without you?

My pudgy hands had picked a pen many, many years ago, but courage, I picked when my mother furtively put up a piece of mine on social media. That courage led me to write to Mr Ramesh Vinayak, who didn't publish me right away, but told me in a way only he can, that I had a flair for writing, and I shouldn't give it up. Over the next few months, my published pieces began to trickle in, and it led me to discover a new side to my father. Not only would he read and re-read those 600-odd words written by his daughter, but he would ensure all his WhatsApp contacts, neighbours, relatives and golf-buddies read them too! My heartfelt thanks to Mama and Papa for helping me discover my love for the pen, and Vinayak sir, for helping me blossom as a writer for the 'Spice of Life' column in *Hindustan Times.*

Thank you to my parents-in-law, who wholeheartedly accepted that their daughter-in-law and her laptop came as a package! Thank you, Mama, for your support and Papa, for sharing your beautiful collection of encyclopedias and books on Sikh history and religion.

Thank you, my dear daughters, for keenly listening and suppressing yawns, as I read aloud, my book draft night after night. You, and so many other children like you all over the world are the force behind the idea of this book. 'Mama, when can we hold the "real" book in our hands?' is what egged me to meet deadlines. Thank you, girls.

Thank you Gurfateh, my partner and best friend, for not being merely a figment of my imagination, but for being a real, almost-utopian millennial husband I thought only existed in rom-coms.

Chandigarh Literary Society helped me meet Mr Vivek Atray, who would inadvertently begin conversation with, 'When is the writer turning into an author?' Thank you Vivek sir, the journey has been as special as you'd promised. A big thank you to Mr Pankaj of The Browser, whose calm demeanour and poise never let expose the high-pressure that the process of publishing can be. Of course, there were several to-and-fros, but the polished version you have in your hands, is a product of his meticulous precision. Of course, a deep sense of gratitude to the world of Instagram, for helping me find Anantjeet, a brilliant illustrator, whose constant question – 'For whom are you writing, again?' – made me discover so much about my own deep-set beliefs and what I wanted through this book. Thank you, Anant!

Thank you, dear reader, for picking this book and giving it space in your library and in your hearts. As you read through its pages, I hope it gives you the same sense of peace and pride I had while penning it.

The biggest gratitude to the amazing heroes who have paved the path for the rest of us, and made the journey easier. One book cannot do justice to so many amazing Sikhs. This is just the beginning. Thank you for being our heritage, our inspiration, our blueprint for how lives are meant to be lived.

— Seerat Kaur Gill

Meet the Creators!

Seerat Kaur Gill

Author

Seerat Kaur Gill is an Electronics and Communication engineer, with a Masters in Management from Warwick Business School (UK). She returned to India and worked in the field of education before plunging into a PhD. As a doctorate in higher education and quality management, publishing academic papers is a part of her work now.

However, she believes that writing life stories and articles is her true calling. Seerat writes for *The Tribune*, *Hindustan Times*, *The Hindu*, *Times of India* and *The Huffington Post*. She lives in a quintessential Punjabi, happy, joint family, which is almost an oxymoron. ***One Amazing Sikh at a Time*** is her first book, whose idea was triggered by a series of events, and its underlying force has been her two daughters and their relentless demand for endless bedtime stories.

On days when she's not writing, she's diligently reading out articles to her husband, who in ten years of marriage, has set himself into a wonderful routine of nodding and cheering in appropriate measure.

Anantjeet Kaur

Illustrator

Anantjeet Kaur is an independent illustrator and graphic designer from Delhi. She graduated in graphic design and English literature. Her curiosity and deep love for adventure & travel takes her across the length and breadth of her country as often as time permits.

Before being mentored by stalwarts at the Riyaaz Academy in illustration for children's books, she worked with design studios, did a short stint as a production assistant for light & sound shows and volunteered at a school for children with special needs. A varied life experience (however short) and love for her country as well as her Sikh roots propel her imagination in a unique way.

Often spotted sketching during kirtan in a gurudwara, drawing is her way to make sense of her surroundings. When not sketching, she surreptitiously observes children and tries to live life just as uninhibited.